One Year After F.I.R.E.

Tinu Publishing, LLC

ISBN 978-0-9863204-5-3

EBOOK ISBN 9780986320446

One Year After F.I.R.E.

Stories and Lessons Learned in Early Retirement

A short memoir

by

Ramat Oyetunji

Other books by Ramat Oyetunji

→ Fifty Shades of Green: A Stock Market Guide

→ Kids and Money: The 5 Stacks Method

→ Transform Your Finances: 28 Days to Better Financial Wellness

Dedication

This book is dedicated to my family and friends. I am grateful for their support, and their unwavering confidence in me.

Special thanks to my daughter, who is amazing in every way.

Me and my daughter at Thanksgiving, 2022

About Me

I am the Founder & CEO of The FI Woman, LLC, a Financial Wellness & Literacy company. I am a Certified Personal Finance Counselor and author of several books.

I retired in 2021 at 44, and after one year of retirement, I wanted to share my experience to encourage and inspire others on their financial journey. By the end of this book, you will have learned a lot more about me!

CONTENTS

PROLOGUE

My Journey to Early Retirement

I looked up from my laptop and made eye contact with an elderly gentleman seated at a table across from mine. I smiled at him, and he smiled back.

"You look like you're working on something important," he said.

"I am working on the outline of a book. But it's still in the early stages."

He smiled and didn't probe further, for which I was grateful because I did not feel like talking about the book. Yet.

As I sat in my local Barnes & Noble store writing, I noticed that I was mostly surrounded by two types of people: people who appeared to be in their 60s or older, and those whom I guessed were students. Mainly, the bookstore was mostly empty. Not surprising, considering I was in there at 10 AM on a workday.

I continued to scan the store during writing breaks and saw the occasional parent with a young child. Usually Mom, but sometimes Dad too. I saw someone who looked like they were having a meeting with a new client; they were brief and parted ways shortly. What I didn't see was anyone who looked like they had skipped work to spend the day at a bookstore. I sometimes wondered if that's how I appeared to others.

You see, on July 2, 2021, I officially retired. At age 44.

One week before my last day at CRC, my daughter and I attended a company event at the Pocono Raceway. It was the perfect sendoff.

I was 44 years old and had worked in a full-time, professional capacity for more than 20 years.

In a way, I had been planning for this day since 2011 and, in what seemed like the blink of an eye, the day arrived a year earlier than I originally planned.

In 2011, I was dissatisfied with my career and work life. I had very little job fulfillment and only fleeting job satisfaction. I started plotting ways to escape. I had always wanted to own a bookstore or some other business where I could have discussions and exchange ideas with others, but I didn't dare to jump into entrepreneurship without a safety net. At the time, I was earning $85K annually and I was a DINK, but I still didn't feel I could give up that income to plunge into the tumultuous and uncertain world of entrepreneurship.

Side note: DINK stands for Dual Income No Kids. According to a Wikipedia entry "The term was coined at the height of yuppie culture in the 1980s. The Great Recession solidified this social trend, as more couples waited longer to have children or chose not to have children at all."

2011 turned out to be a pivotal point in my financial independence journey, and I became serious about achieving financial Independence. One of the first steps I took was scrapping our plan to buy a single-family home, and instead, we bought a duplex so that we could earn rental income. Later, I would buy three more investment properties on my own.

Real estate investing played a pivotal role in my ability to retire early, and I credit it to reading Robert Kiyosaki's *The Cash Flow Quadrant: A Guide to Financial Freedom.*

From then on, I read other real estate investing books, scouted properties, learned to quickly assess a property's viability based on my criteria, viewed homes for sale on sites like Zillow daily, and even used weekends to drive through neighborhoods to get a feel for the area.

In one of the earliest entries in my "Big Book of Dreams" journal, I detailed my long-term goals. It was dated May 22, 2011, and I had set a target date of February 26, 2017, to accomplish the goals. The entry read:

→ Passive income > $100,000/yr.

→ Rental properties with positive cash flow

→ A business system generating cash flow

→ No longer an employee

→ A successful business owner and investor

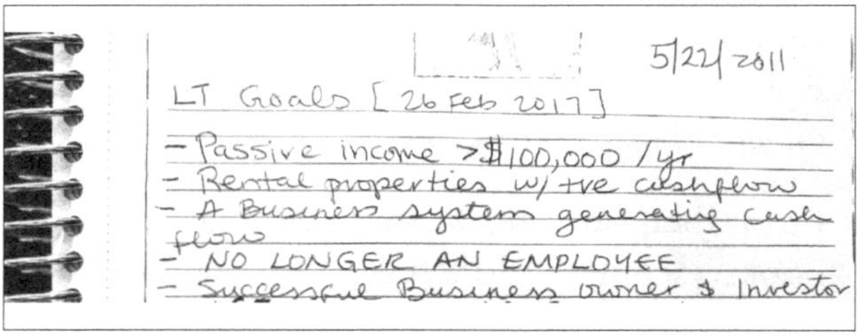
5/22/2011

LT Goals [26 Feb 2017]

- Passive income >$100,000 /yr
- Rental properties w/ +ve cashflow
- A Business system generating cash flow
- NO LONGER AN EMPLOYEE
- Successful Business owner & Investor

My earliest entry outlining my long-term financial goals.

I remember writing those words with a lot of hope and uncertainty in 2011. I didn't know how I would make those goals happen. Working for a pharma company with an engineering degree and an MBA, I earned a decent wage, but I knew it wasn't enough to get me to financial independence. How did I think I would be able to make six figures in passive income? It seemed daunting, unlikely, and overly optimistic.

I wish I could say in this book that after writing so many iterations of my long-term goals, I buckled down, made concrete plans, and executed them flawlessly. I would love to say that, but it wouldn't be true. As with any plan, and any journey, it's never a straight line to the finish. There are bumps in the road, hurdles, and obstacles to overcome.

From 2011, when I started writing my escape plan aka financial goals until I retired in 2021, a lot of life happened. I got pregnant and my daughter was born in 2012, we moved from the duplex, and I experienced many role changes and a company change.

As life happened, there were years when I revisited and revised the plan. For example, after the birth of my daughter, I revised my target date from Feb 26, 2017, to February 26, 2022, when I would turn 45. There were other years when I operated on autopilot and didn't think of or revise my plan at all. What remained consistent was making decisions that moved me toward the goals I outlined.

In the summer of 2020, I came to a startling realization. I had accumulated enough assets to support my expenses, based on the 4% rule.

Side note: A Forbes article published in 2022 explains the 4% rule thus "In the first year of retirement, you can withdraw up to 4% of your portfolio's value. If you have $1 million saved for retirement, for example, you could spend $40,000 in the first year of retirement following the 4% rule. After the first year, you must adjust your withdrawals each year for inflation."

I had technically reached financial independence, though it did not match what I had written in my journal in 2011. Instead, it met and exceeded a visual representation that I made in 2014. At the time, I visualized a path to financial independence, printed it and posted it on a vision board that I looked at every day for motivation.

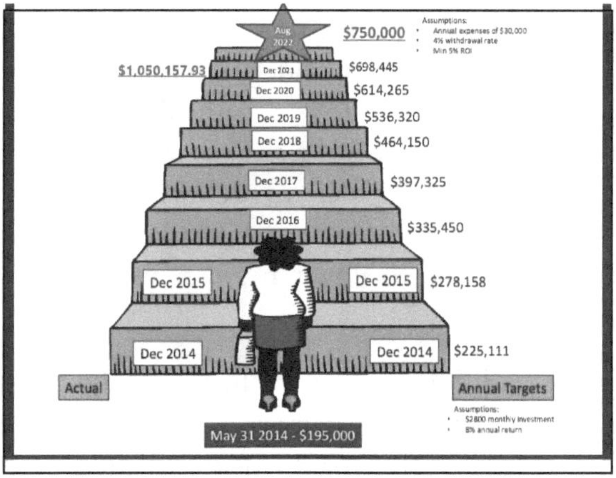

In 2014 I visualized a path to Financial Independence. In 2021, I updated the left side of the pyramid to reflect my actual portfolio value.

On my journey to financial independence, I have focused on two main things: eliminating debt and accumulating assets that have the potential to provide an income. Although by the time I retired I was earning $155K, excluding bonuses, I knew that the minimum income I needed to cover my expenses, including built-in self-care and fun items, was $40K. So, I knew I had reached financial independence when my assets could generate an annual income of $40K. It wasn't my 2011 goal of $100K in passive income, but it met my definition of financial independence; the ability to generate enough income to cover my expenses without working.

I took additional steps to further solidify my position; from the summer of 2020 until I retired in July 2021, I paid off my car and credit cards, I accumulated enough cash to ensure I was liquid for at least the first few years of retirement without tapping into investment accounts, and I took advantage of rising property valuations to reduce my investment property holdings.

But after all that planning and execution, the decision to FIRE in the summer of 2021 wasn't based on my preparedness. Instead, it was influenced by unforeseen circumstances that I will describe next.

Side note: FIRE is an acronym for Financial Independence Retire Early. An Investopedia article describes it as "A movement of people devoted to a program of extreme savings and investment that aims to allow them to retire far earlier than traditional budgets and retirement plans would permit." There are other descriptions of what FIRE is and what it means. In the end, you define your criteria for FIRE and how you achieve it.

MY FIRE JOURNEY TIMELINE

May 2001: College Graduation

Graduated college with a BS in Mechanical Engineering and a minor in Business.

July 2001: First "real" Job

Excited to start my first job with Schlumberger Ltd. as an Offshore Field Engineer.

Salary: $51,600/yr. plus bonuses.

Feb 2002: Casualty of Layoffs

The ripple effects of 9/11 and storms in the Gulf of Mexico led to layoffs in the Oil & Gas industry.

Good news: I had just paid off my credit card debt and started a savings account.

Bad news: I had a Ford Mustang with a monthly payment, foreign national status, and less than $2K in savings.

Aug 2002: Grad School

Started Grad school on a Graduate Assistantship that covered tuition, room and board, and provided a $600 monthly stipend.

Good news: sold my mustang and bought a used Jetta. Now, I was debt-free!

Opened an ING Direct account and, from my $600 monthly stipend, started investing $100/month and put $100/month in a savings account.

May 2005: Graduation and Re-entry into the Workforce

Graduated with an MBA and started working full-time at P&G, earning $71,500/yr.

Started contributing to my 401(k) and increased my monthly ING investments from $100 to $500.

2008 – 2009: Career Pivot to Pursue My Passion

Became a licensed Financial Advisor at Edward Jones Investments.

Excited to learn about investing and wealth-building strategies to help people grow their money. Gained invaluable knowledge about the stock market and other investments.

Sep 2008: a casualty of another layoff, this time primarily driven by the real-estate and banking meltdown.

Apr 2009: Back to Engineering. Started a new job at Merck, earning $80K/yr.

2011: Getting "real" with FI

Purchased the first of 4 investment properties: a duplex instead of a single-family home.

First written plan to achieve financial independence by 2022 at age 45.

2015: The FI Woman

Launched The FI Woman, LLC as a Registered Investment Advisor firm to teach women how to invest in the stock market and achieve financial independence.

At the time, I viewed The FI Woman as a passion project to provide educational content, and not as a source of income.

Published the first of three personal finance books, "Fifty Shades of Green: A Stock Market Guide."

2021: Retired at 44!

Final salary: $155K/yr. + bonuses.

Target retirement income: $40K/yr.

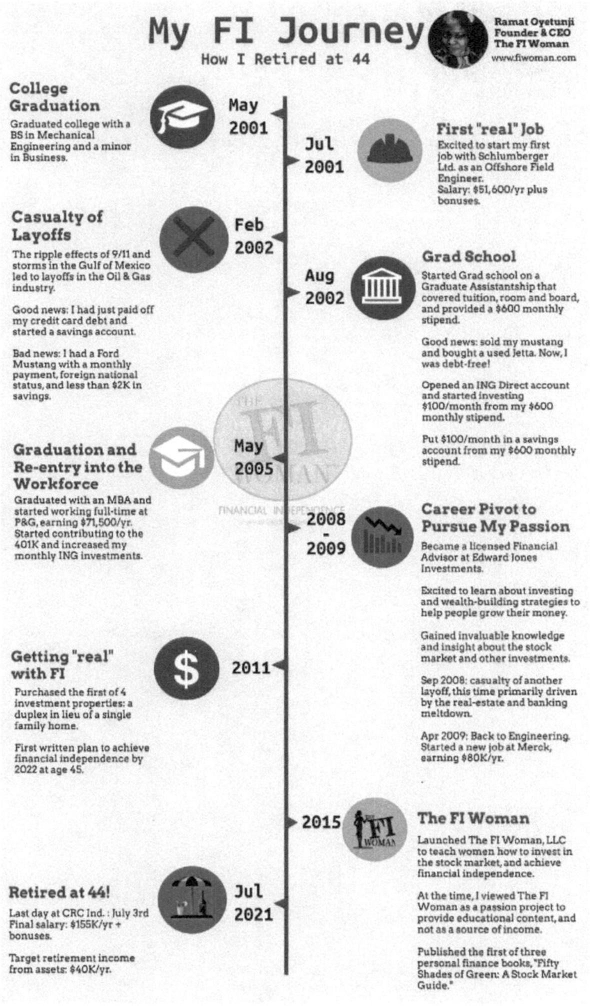

Illustration of my FIRE journey timeline.

PART ONE

How The Pandemic Accelerated My FIRE Journey

"It's no worse than the flu," one colleague said while we were getting coffee from the breakroom.

It was March 6, 2020, and the word "Covid" was still alien on our tongues. Earlier that day, my boss and I were in a one-to-one meeting discussing potential supply chain issues and some risk mitigation that we could implement.

Since December 2019 there had been talk of some virus, that to many of us was happening far, far away in China. It was something that we only paid passing attention to, but by that one-to-one in March, it was grabbing more of our attention. My earliest recollection of things getting real was when a local newspaper reported several cases of the virus in my state of residence.

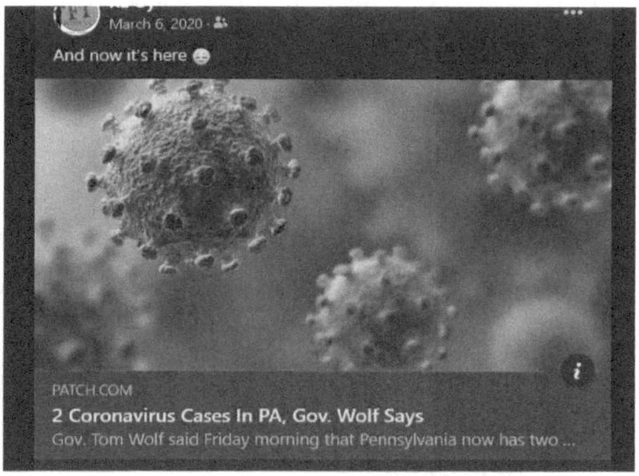

When a local newspaper reported several cases of the virus in my state of residence.

The COVID-19 pandemic affected everyone around the world, and I believe that we still don't know the full impact - mentally, physically, and emotionally- it has had on those of us who survived.

In December 2019, everything looked bright. I started a new job after leaving my previous employer of 10 years. It was a promotion into a challenging, management role. I had heard some rumblings about covid, but at the time, it was something happening far away in China. 2020 started with a bang and life proceeded as usual until March of 2020. The far-away rumblings had spread beyond being a distant problem. It was right at our doorsteps, and we all went into lockdown.

As with most traumatic events, the details, emotions, and feelings of the time have begun to dull as time has passed. I think of it as a dark and chaotic time. I vaguely remember how stressful simple tasks like grocery shopping became, how there was no toilet paper on the shelves, and finding hand sanitizer or Clorox wipes? Dream on. These items were as precious as gold in 2020.

Because of the prolonged chaos of Covid, to this day, I sometimes have a difficult time distinguishing between the happenings of 2020 and 2021 because it felt like one long year instead of two separate years.

At the time of the lockdown, my daughter was in 2nd grade. It felt like one day they were attending school as usual, and then the next thing we knew, the kids were abruptly sent home with laptops and hastily formulated lesson plans. Parents suddenly found themselves in the role of teachers, while teachers tried their best to help both parents and students, even as they were dealing with their own lives being disrupted by covid and the lockdown. What was initially a two-week lockdown extended to the rest of the school year, and for some families, into the following school year too.

"I wish we could go back to the days when we were free."

That was a comment my daughter made one day in April during the lockdown. She was seven at the time and I'm sure it felt that her whole world had changed drastically. It was during this period that we discovered interactive video games like Roblox, as a way for the kids to connect with their friends that they could no longer see or visit. Sadly, even after the lockdown was lifted, the hold Roblox and video games had on my daughter remained.

Almost two weeks after "it got real" people all over the world were trying to stay positive; there were news stories of people in lockdown singing from balconies, and there were hilarious memes aplenty. There were fewer jokes as days turned into weeks and the world remained in lockdown.

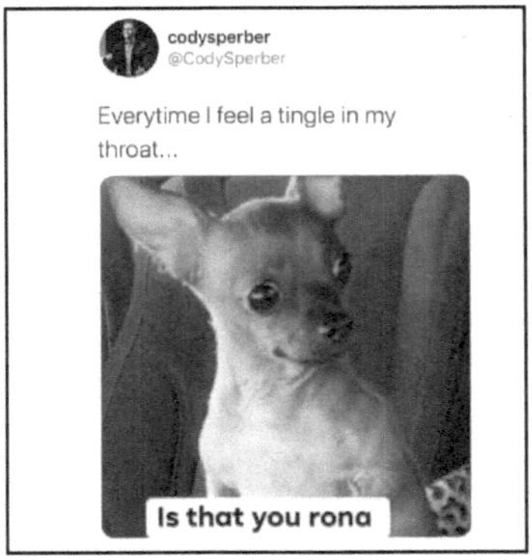

My Facebook post from March 18, 2020, when we were still optimistic and joking about Covid.

Lockdown wasn't all bad. I got a taste of what early retirement could be like. One bright and vivid memory still lingers. While the schools were physically closed and kids were going to school remotely, I started a fun ritual with my daughter. At 10 AM every day, we would go for a walk around our neighborhood and into the adjacent neighborhoods. On one such morning walk, I remember how empty the streets were, and the calm stillness in the air. It was so tranquil, and I briefly wished it could stay that way for a long time. It couldn't of course, but we enjoyed those moments from the 2020 lockdown, and it's one of the memories I cherish from that period.

That memory and having a lot of time with my daughter because we were all stuck indoors, helped paint a picture of what retirement life could be like.

Aha moment: *Getting a taste of the future goes a long way in helping you visualize and accelerate it.*

If 2020 was a period of chaos and adjustment, then I would say 2021 was a period of consequences.

Starting in 2021, my extended family experienced a series of health crises connected with the pandemic. While writing this book, I tried to recall the intense feelings and stress that my family and I went through from January to the end of April 2021. But as with all traumatic events, the passage of time has dulled the memories and feelings from the time. I do recall, sleepless nights, worrying, trying to be present for my daughter who was still remote learning, trying to be present at work for my team and the company, and needing to solve the problems the pandemic had thrown our way.

One morning, after a particularly long night of phone calls with doctors who were in a different time zone, I was attending a virtual meeting and fell asleep! Fortunately, it was a meeting where I was a listener, not a contributor, so my presence wasn't missed. Even so, I was mortified and upset. It was one of many wake-up calls I received.

My health suffered. My mental, physical, and emotional states were impacted. My outlook on life and what was important changed. My thoughts about retiring changed.

Although in 2020 I realized I could support my expenses with the assets I had accumulated, I hadn't thought of retiring yet. I enjoyed what I did for a living, I enjoyed earning a six-figure income, and I figured I could continue earning, saving, and investing to provide an additional cushion in retirement.

But after pulling through the crisis, I realized I was heading for a major breakdown. I considered taking a leave of absence from work to help me reset, overcome the effects of dealing with the family crisis, and give myself time to find my place in the "new normal" of life post-Covid. My boss at the time was supportive of a leave of absence, but ultimately, I concluded that it would not give me the space and time that I truly needed. I knew that I would still worry about my team, I would be anxious about the best time to return, and even more anxious if I needed to extend the leave of absence. I realized that the leave of absence would become a form of mental stress, instead of helping me find peace. So, I decided to retire.

***Aha moment**: Sometimes you are more ready than you think you are, and with all the planning in the world, it still requires a leap of faith to make a bold move.*

PART TWO

THE WHIRLWIND SUMMER OF 2021

Retirement began with a relaxing trip to Maine for the summer. On my first morning after retirement, I woke up to this amazing view.

"Lobstah" … Quintessential Maine summer fare!

I hesitated to tell people I had retired because it seemed absurd. When I casually mentioned it to a few people they gave polite nods or blank looks, and it was clear they didn't "get it."

I was particularly hesitant to tell my parents. My father had worked for the same company his entire career until retirement. I felt that they wouldn't understand why I would give up a career and well-paying job during my peak earning years.

I should have trusted them more. Their response was amazing. I shared their reaction with a friend in the following text message:

"On Sunday I told my parents about retiring and running my business full-time starting in July. Their reaction was amazing. I'd been dragging my feet about telling them because I imagined they wouldn't get it and wouldn't understand leaving a good

job, etc. Instead, they were full of encouragement and so PROUD!

On the call they already built up my business, describing what it could become. I could hear their pride and faith in me through the call. They had zero doubt that I would succeed, and they said with 100% certainty "we know you've done the necessary evaluation."

They also asked how they could help, for example, promote/spread the word. It was amazing."

Most reactions to my retirement were more positive than negative. I think part of my hesitation in talking about my retirement was feeling like a fraud. Can I really call this retirement?

It didn't help that a social media exchange one day further highlighted my self-doubt.

"I am sick and tired of these stories where people claim to be retired. You are not retired, you just changed jobs from working for someone to working for yourself. You are not living

off your investments, so how can you claim to be retired?"

I felt some vitriol and bitterness from the challenger. I knew she wasn't being objective, after all, she knew nothing about my financial situation or the fact that not only was I living off my investments, but so was my business! It was obvious that she was speaking from her assumptions of my situation, but her words stung and did nothing to minimize my feelings of being a fraud.

Aha moment: *Reaction to my early retirement has very little to do with me, and more to do with that person, their mindset, and their beliefs. How I take their reaction depends entirely on how I feel about my retirement.*

"SWEET TREAT"

At the beginning of my retirement, I experienced what I imagine any newly retired person experiences; I found it hard to relax. After years of working, achieving goals, receiving accolades, and focusing on getting results, it was ingrained in me to wake up with goals and a list of things I wanted to accomplish that day or that week. So instead of the sleep-in and do-whatever-I-want retirement I imagined, I approached retirement with gusto and a desire to do everything.

For the first time, I was going to be able to spend the entire summer with my daughter without her going to summer camp, or me going to work. I was excited and the thought and started filling our days with activities. A lot of activities.

"I came across this virtual baking summer camp. It looks like fun! Anyone interested?"

I came across a virtual baking summer camp for kids 9-14 that looked absolutely adorable. It was for five days, Monday to Friday, from 12:30 – 4:30 PM. It had a leadership component where the kids discussed positive body image and being an entrepreneur. That made it even more attractive to me as an opportunity for my daughter to do something fun, meet other amazing kids, and learn some important lessons. I sent a link for the camp to friends, hoping they would enroll their kids as a fun group activity. Most friends couldn't sign their kids for a variety of reasons, the timing being one of them. Fortunately, one of my daughter's closest friends signed up, and I offered to host her at our house so that they could work together and have pre-camp or post-camp play dates. It was a total win-win because it meant a more engaging camp experience for both girls. The best part was because they needed some adult supervision, I got to pseudo-participate in their activities.

It was a delight getting to watch my daughter and her friend without any distractions. The kitchen was a mess after each camp activity, but unlike before, it wasn't nerve-wracking or stress-inducing. I knew I had the time to clean up and it wasn't going to take up the little time I had or compete with the time that I needed to complete work. It was a mental load off my mind not to worry about time, and that allowed me to relax and fully immerse myself in the time spent with the girls.

I even had the time and energy to say yes when they suggested that at the end of every day, they would set up a small baked goods stand in front of the house. We had fun arranging the goods and making signs. I didn't have to worry about taking time away from work or planning the next meeting, and I even sat outside with them, chatting with neighbors that walked by.

It was a memorable part of our summer.

Aha moment: *The mental and psychological aspect of knowing that you have control of your time is underestimated. That psychological freedom opened my mind to a variety of joyful actions that I had previously not allowed myself to experience or indulge in.*

First day of camp: meeting other campers. Notice the kitchen is still relatively clean and orderly!

Clean and orderly quickly went out the window!

Day 3: Making cupcakes from scratch. They were delish.

The girls got to express their creativity.

Budding entrepreneurs! Selling their baked goods to neighbors.

Baking summer camp was fun, and a success!

"Life Skills and Money Lessons"

One of the highlights of our whirlwind summer was helping my daughter start a business. Here's how it began.

One summer afternoon my daughter and I were walking around our neighborhood. It was a sunny day, the sky was clear with a few clouds lazily floating by, and there was a nice breeze. My daughter was 8 at the time and her 9th birthday was in a few weeks.

"After our walk, I can play Roblox, right?"

I wasn't particularly thrilled about her parking herself in front of the computer for the rest of the afternoon, so I thought of a chore to keep her a bit occupied.

"Actually, you need to clean my car because you have made it a mess!"

During the walk, she asked if I would pay her to clean my car. I paused to think about it and then promised her that I would pay her if she went above and beyond just "picking up." I didn't have any expectations beyond her just picking up, to be honest, but I could see the wheels turning as she asked more questions. I was beyond impressed when by the end of the walk, she was suggesting that we sign a contract before she started the job!

She went right to work once we got home. She spent more than two hours vacuuming, wiping, and scrubbing. I had never seen her work so hard! I was impressed enough to pay her and give her a big tip. But she didn't stop there. She wrote a business plan in PowerPoint and came up with a slogan:

"Car a mess? Don't stress!"

That was the beginning of her car cleaning business.

Before long, she had a few customers from the neighborhood.

Starting a business and earning money allowed her to learn important money lessons, which we turned into a kid's book about money. After the book was published, she was featured in a local paper, and hosted two book signing events: one at a popular local bookstore and the other at our local Barnes & Noble. More on that later.

***Aha moment**: There was a side of my daughter that I would never have discovered without the opportunity to spend so much unstructured time with her. A lot of deep conversations and insights into her mind happened in passing and would never have happened previously when we were on a timetable or scheduled time.*

"Epic Adventures"

The summer was filled with a variety of adventures from camping trips to a visit to UNC Durham, and a road trip from Pennsylvania to Kentucky, with stops in Pittsburgh and Columbus, Ohio.

We were still restricted by Covid so many of our summer plans were local, outdoors and with as few people as possible. Even so, we were able to make the most of it.

Having the freedom to spend as much time as I wished during these trips made a huge difference, and since my daughter was on her summer break from school, she became my willing travel companion.

I spent so much uninterrupted, quality time with her that summer. It was unforgettable, and we created memories that I'll forever cherish.

One of our first stops during our epic summer road trip was Pittsburgh, Pennsylvania.

A one-of-a-kind cafe in Pittsburgh

Night view of Columbus, Ohio. During our whirl-wind summer, an epic road trip included a visit to a very dear friend from college. I got to meet her kids for the first time, and they met my daughter. By the end of the trip, they were semi-besties!

Scioto mile in Columbus provided amazing night views of the city, and fun on electric scooters!

Camping at a state park in Pennsylvania

One of the spectacular waterfalls in a Pennsylvania state park.

"The Cave" A fire station built into the hills. Our epic road trip ended in Lexington, KY to visit with my parents.

Spotted in Durham, North Carolina. We visited towards the end of summer to help my niece move into her dorm as a freshman at UNC.

"There is a whole new kind of life ahead, full of experiences just waiting to happen. Some call it 'retirement.' I call it bliss." –Betty Sullivan

PART THREE

Euphoria, Fear, Loneliness

The Euphoria Phase

Merriam Webster definition of euphoria: a feeling of well-being or elation.

"Yes, I can help!"

"Yes, I will lead that!"

"No problem, my schedule is flexible."

Euphoria is the only way to describe the first 6 months of my retirement. I discovered so many things and signed up for a million and one other things. I was available and up for anything!

After the hectic pace of my first summer in retirement, the school year began, and with it, an introduction to a whole new world of school volunteering and involvement. Don't get me wrong, before retiring I volunteered for as many school activities as I could, especially ones involving my daughter. But now, I was going beyond signing up for a task on a signup genius, to being the person who organized the event and created the signup genius. I learned that there is a big difference between the two.

I signed up for everything I could at my daughter's school from a class parent, to book fair chair, to soccer snack stand, to reading Olympics. You name it, and I was there. Suddenly, I was "that parent" I had previously wondered about. I wondered how that parent, typically a mom, had the time to get involved in all the school activities. I often wondered if they were SAHMs because I couldn't fathom how they found the energy to organize school events and also work a full job. Not to mention that many activities happened in the middle of the workday when many parents couldn't always get away from work.

That was pre-retirement me. Retirement me was pretty much available and up for anything. That 9:15 AM parade at the school? Count me in and you can also count on me taking lots of pics! How about the Home & School Association meeting, the one that starts at 7 PM after you've had an exhausting day at work, and goes on till 9 PM as discussions drag on about activities and fundraisers? Sure, count me in!

Before I retired, whenever I volunteered at the school, I felt connected and happy that I was making time and getting involved. I felt fortunate to have flexible roles, and I didn't notice until after retirement that I was never fully relaxed or fully present during those times. There was always the nagging thought of the work I had to do next, or the return drive ahead of me or making sure I wasn't out of the office too long. I didn't notice that nagging feeling until after retiring, and I noticed that I was experiencing the same activities differently.

This time, there were no nagging thoughts about work, the team, a meeting, or the drive back. I could just relax, go with the flow, enjoy the moments, and even prolong my time at the event on a whim. The difference between my experience now and my experience from before was palpable, but I would never have realized what I was missing.

Picked up my daughter and her friends from school one Tuesday for an impromptu "Boba Tea" play date.

The dictionary defines headspace as a person's state of mind or mindset, and further elaborates that headspace focuses on "the capacity to think clearly, without interference."

I didn't realize how much of my energy and headspace was dedicated to work, work-related thoughts, conflicts, and problems. I didn't realize it because it had become my normal mode of functioning, and only when I was no longer in that mode was I able to realize what I was missing all along. I had been missing the energy and headspace to experience the other things happening in my life. But now, I had the energy and headspace to experience more of my life, especially my daughter's life, instead of experiencing the fringes of it as I had done in the past.

Aha moment: *we don't always know what experiences we are not fully enjoying until we free up the energy and headspace to experience them differently.*

"The Book Fair and School Garden"

While still in my euphoric phase, one of the rewarding and fulfilling things I enjoyed about getting more involved at my daughter's school was the diversity I brought to the meetings, committees, and events. I discovered how much effort and love the parent volunteer groups pour into creating an enriching experience at the school, but I also learned that there was low participation in the planning committees, the ones that did the heavy lifting, and there was very little diversity. I was happy to help in improving that. Not only were the other committee members happy to see a fresh face, I think the students liked it too. An interaction during the spring book fair stood out to me.

I volunteered to chair the school's book fair event in the spring. When I volunteered in January, I didn't know what I was getting into, but

I knew I had the time and energy to give the event my best shot. It is an event that lasts the entire week, provides an enriching experience for students, and raises money for niceties at the school. Though the event lasts only a week, it takes four months of intense planning to pull it off! I was fortunate to have the former chair as a guide and the help of many awesome parent volunteers. It was all worth it to see the wonder and delight on the kids' faces as they walked into a classroom that had been transformed into a fun space with books, posters, and decorations.

During the week-long event, I noticed that as classes cycled through, the kids were particularly interested in me. They would steal glances my way, smile, stare, and some would screw up enough courage to ask if I was so-and-so's mother. I stood out because there weren't many people of color among the staff, teachers, or parent volunteers.

I was delighted by their curiosity and attention! I loved engaging with the kids and indulging in their questions. I especially loved it when one little girl of color looked at me adoringly and didn't let go of my hand for the entirety of her class's visit.

I encountered similar experiences volunteering in the school garden, where I was able to interact with the kids outside, and wow them with tales of how big the yams in Nigeria are compared to the ones they are familiar with. During one such garden session, I even came across a little 3rd-grade boy who told me his mom was from Nigeria and he proudly shared the things he knew about it.

These school and community activities have been one of the more fulfilling and delightful experiences since retiring.

A classroom transformed for the Book Fair

The school garden where I volunteer weekly and get the opportunity to see my daughter in a different element. A huge bonus is getting to work with so many delightful kids in different grades.

Sights and harvests from one of my volunteer days in the school.

"Writing And Publishing Two Books"

I was operating in high drive during my first six months in retirement. I wanted to do and experience everything! Towards the end of 2021, my daughter and I started writing a book based on her experience from starting a business, and in November 2021, we published her first book *Kids and Money: The 5 Stacks Method.*

.In an earlier section, I described how she started a car cleaning business because she wanted to earn money to buy Robux, an in-game currency for Roblox. As her business grew and she earned more money, she naturally wanted to spend it all. I'm sure it comes as no surprise that I wasn't going to let that happen!

One night, she requested a bedtime story, insisting that it should be one I had made up myself. It wasn't an uncommon request from her, and I thought it was the perfect opportunity for me to weave a tale of financial savvy. I created a fictional character who was my daughter's age and who had also just started a business. I described how this character managed her money smartly by dividing it into five stacks, each with a purpose.

"Should I be like her and divide my money into five stacks too?"

When she asked that question, I knew that my plan had worked, and The 5 Stacks Method was born. It helped her think of money differently and smartly manage the money she was earning from her business. As I shared the story with friends and on social media, I got feedback about how useful the information would be to other kids, so we decided to publish a book just for kids. It was another great opportunity for us to bond differently.

We spent many months writing a book to help kids learn to be smart with money.

Beautiful sign for my daughter's book signing at Barnes and Noble.

While working on *Kids and Money: The 5 Stacks Method*, I was inspired to write an adult version; a step-by-step guide to help adults manage their money and improve their financial wellness.

Long before I launched The FI Woman, I had served as an informal financial sounding board to friends and family members. I shared my story and knowledge with them, but many times they didn't act. I found it curious that they wanted to improve their finances but struggled to take the necessary steps. How could I help to change that?

Working with my daughter to write the kids' book helped me realize that simple, manageable steps were the answer. I went straight to work writing a book that provided step-by-step guidance and designed it as a daily planner with images to keep readers engaged. Writing *Transform Your Finances* gave me purpose and was uniquely challenging because I was trying to break complex topics into small steps that were easy for most people to understand, and simple enough to follow.

In January 2022 I published *Transform Your Finances*. It's a complete guide that anyone can use to get started or improve their finances. I poured my knowledge into it with the genuine desire to help others take control of their money. I sent a copy to my dad, and after he read through it thoroughly – he has a PhD in Electrical Engineering and being thorough is second nature! – he said, "anyone who follows the steps in this book will definitely improve their finances." That was all the validation I needed.

My first six months in retirement, from July to December, were hectic but satisfying. I did a lot and accomplished a lot in a very short span. I probably did more in those six months than I would have if I wasn't retired, but it didn't feel like work, and that's a major difference!

***Aha moment**: when I am working on the things that matter most to me, it doesn't feel like work.*

TRANSFORM YOUR FINANCES

TAKE CONTROL OF YOUR MONEY

28 DAYS TO BETTER FINANCIAL WELLNESS

DAILY PLANNER

RAMAT OYETUNJI

Transform Your Finances was challenging and fulfilling to write, and I am proud of how it turned out. It is detailed, easy to understand and follow.

Fear Takes Hold

Merriam Webster definition of fear: anxious concern.

"It was so nice not having to think about money."

This thought popped into my head as I was looking at one of my accounts with less than $500 in it. Someone needed financial assistance and I promised to send $500. It wasn't the first time I had lent a helping hand to friends, relatives, and sometimes strangers via an appealing GoFundMe campaign. But it was the first time that I didn't have $500 in an account that I could send without hesitation. I checked in on several other accounts and found they had low balances too. I eventually made multiple transfers and sent the money.

It dawned on me that I could no longer view and spend money as I had done in the past. Since retiring, money felt more finite, like a very limited resource. Before I retired, money felt like a renewable resource because every two weeks my account was replenished, and even if it was just psychological, I never really felt I would run out of money.

I no longer have that same laisse affair feeling.

Retirement has given me a newfound respect and appreciation for money. It is humbling, but also a great lesson that I appreciate.

Aha moment: *It is easy to be generous when you have a lot, but when you don't, generosity takes intention and can feel more meaningful.*

The stock market took a beating in 2022 and my portfolio was no exception!

I shared an image of my portfolio in a private personal finance group, and some of the comments reflected my inner fears, even though my rational side was fighting to prevail.

My rational side said all the right things:

"Don't look at your portfolio"

"Stay the course"

"Stick to your investment plan"

All sage advice that I technically knew and understood.

Plus, this wasn't my first rodeo with a sharply declining stock market; I lived through the stock market crash of 2008. But there was one big difference this time around: I am retired.

In 2008 I was 31 and working. I had a few hundred thousand invested in the stock market and a long horizon. I was also a financial advisor with Edward Jones at the time, with a lot of resources and "industry elders" to help me understand and weather the storm.

This time, it felt different because I have more to lose. My million-dollar portfolio rapidly declined. I wasn't working or contributing to a 401(k) or IRA and so I couldn't console myself with the time-tested "I'm buying shares on sale thanks to Dollar Cost Averaging." I was working with a fixed lump sum that was rapidly getting decimated.

Some of the euphoria I described in the earlier section also extended itself into my investing, and against my better judgement, I had used some of my cash to buy "shares on sale."

Needless to say, before long, the shares were further discounted!

Even the typical consolation of "I'm buying quality stocks/investments and I am in it for the long run" didn't offer any consolation as every listed company seemed to be testing new 52-week lows.

I was genuinely worried that I was going to have to "unretire" just one year into retirement!

The fear was real enough that I even looked at jobs on LinkedIn and half-heartedly applied to one or two. No surprises when I didn't get any calls back, I mean, I didn't even bother with a resume or cover letter, I just sent them my LinkedIn profile. Yikes!

My fear was peaking by the time a friend reached out to me about a tempting opportunity.

"The Offer"

I was intrigued. I hadn't spoken to this friend in years, though we passively stay in touch on social media. What could the opportunity possibly be?

The following day I called him, and the conversation threw me for a loop! He wanted to know if I was interested in returning as a licensed Financial Advisor and joining his office.

He is a successful Financial Advisor with millions of dollars in Assets Under Management. He has the perfect personality for a successful Financial Advisor: smart, outgoing, and customer focused.

Side note: Assets Under Management (AUM) is the total market value of the investments that a person or entity manages for investors.

He explained that he is focusing on regional activities and was looking to transfer some of his clients to a financial advisor he could trust. He shared all the positive ways in which the industry and his company in particular had changed.

One of the biggest changes, he explained, is that new advisors are now paid an above-average salary for four years, instead of relying only on commission. In addition to that, unlike when he and I first started as financial advisors, I would be starting with a book of clients, and close to $10 million in AUM.

During our two-hour discussion, he was candid about how I would have to stop some of the work I am doing with my business, The FI Woman. But he also pointed out that I would have the opportunity to work towards becoming a Certified Financial Planner (CFP), a designation I have coveted for a few years.

We wrapped up our meeting and I assured him that I would give his proposal serious thought.

"I am 90% sure I am on board with this opportunity," I told him as we parted ways.

I felt elated on my way home, but there was another surprising feeling lurking under the surface: relief.

"Is this a blessing in disguise?" I asked myself as I drove home.

Is this the answer to the questions, uncertainty, and fear I had been feeling lately?

I mentally ran down all the positives the opportunity offered:

→ Starting in an office with a book of clients, instead of starting from scratch as I had previously done.

→ Having the support of an established company, with systems and processes in place. All I would have to do was follow them diligently.

→ An opportunity to network with others in financial services and make connections that could prove useful if I returned to running my own business.

→ Getting a salary! Getting paid to work in the field I love anyway. I would be able to suspend my retirement spending plan and let my retirement funds grow.

→ Gaining credibility, sales skills, knowledge, and experience that I could later apply to my own business.

→ Finally, an opportunity to work towards the much-coveted CFP designation.

"All I would need to do is put The FI Woman on hold, and work hard in this role for at least the next 5 years."

As I said this to myself, it felt like I was trying to convince myself that it was a good idea. Was it a good idea, or was I letting my fear take over?

I was determined to get it right, and not just talk myself into believing it was a good idea.

I talked it over with my husband, explaining the pros.

"Would you still have the same flexibility that you have now?" He'd gone straight to the crux of the matter.

"It sounds like I would," I replied. I sounded hesitant, even to myself, and his skeptical look confirmed it.

It's true that as a Financial Advisor I would have a flexible work schedule. Advisors are expected to behave like they own the business. But as is to be expected, the firm has expectations and quotas for all Advisors, after all, they want to be profitable!

I texted a friend, another Financial Advisor, who is familiar with the company, the industry, and the work. We scheduled a phone call for the following day.

She listened to the opportunity, and the things that I considered the "pros." She gave me insight into her experience, since joining the firm four years ago. We talked for about thirty minutes.

A couple of days had passed since I first learned about the opportunity, and I was no longer "90% sure."

Instead, I felt closer to "60% sure" it was a good opportunity for me.

Once I let the initial relief subside, I recognized another feeling that had been buried during the initial excitement of hearing about the opportunity: anxiety.

I was anxious at the thought of putting The FI Woman on hold for at least 5 years. I was anxious about unretiring and no longer working at my own pace or on the things that I chose to work on. Wasn't that the very point of achieving financial independence?

I was anxious about going back into a corporate shell and following a ready-made system, albeit a successful and well-established one.

It was interesting to me that the very things that had initially felt comforting and brought a sense of relief, were also the things that were causing some anxiety.

I was coming off the exhilarating and successful completion of The 5 Stacks Camp. My daughter and I had shared four days with amazing campers and I was still feeling euphoric from the experience.

I thought of giving that up, giving up my one-on-one clients, and pausing all the work I was doing to grow my business.

It's true that as a business owner I often feel anxious about wearing so many hats, and building my systems and processes, but I was starting to realize that I found satisfaction and a sense of accomplishment in forging my own way.

The thought of giving that up did not feel good.

By the end of the weekend, I had flipped to "90% sure" that the opportunity wasn't for me, and I felt at peace with it.

***Aha moment**: There is satisfaction and a sense of accomplishment in forging my own way, even when it means being gripped by fear and taking longer to accomplish the things I want.*

Loneliness Sets In

Merriam Webster definition of loneliness: being without company.

As the euphoria of retirement wore off, and the fear subsided, another emotion surfaced: loneliness.

"Thank goodness you make it a point to call me!" I told a friend after one of her many "random calls." She is one of two friends who still prefer calls and doesn't hesitate to pick up the phone when she thinks of you. Before retirement, I appreciated her "just checking in" calls, and since retiring, I consider them a godsend!

It makes sense that many of the people I normally interact with are at work most of the day, and any activity or interaction would be with a different network of people. It makes sense, but I don't think it's something that I or other retirees think about before retiring.

The loneliness came as a surprise because I think of myself as an introvert, one who could remain cooped up inside for many days and be content. But I underestimated the value of the hundreds of interactions I had during a typical day before retirement.

I was surprised to find myself missing the routine of these interactions and starting the day with a predetermined purpose. Although running my business gives me purpose, it's different because I don't have to answer to anyone, I don't have any imposed deadlines or expectations, I don't have to do anything if I don't want to, and when I do, I set my own pace.

Somehow, having that freedom and flexibility wasn't very satisfying, and the reduced interactions only enhanced it.

In the earlier months of retirement, I was so busy with activities and new experiences that I didn't notice the loneliness, or the desire to have some structure. But as my retirement progressed, and everyone else returned to their routine, it became evident.

I decided to create some structure and become more intentional about my interactions and socializing. I could no longer rely on the built-in, automatic socializing that naturally occurs in the workplace and with coworkers.

I developed this basic routine that provided structure, but still maintained flexibility:

7-8:30: Prepping my daughter for school and dropping her off or walking to the bus.

8:30 – 11:00: personal time filled with a variety of activities, including exercise and errands.

12:00 – 4:00: Lunch dates, client meetings, and business-related items.

4:00 – School pick-up.

After 4:00: a variety of tasks sometimes personal, family, or business-related.

It's still too early to call the loneliness problem solved, so I plan to continue tuning in, to see if the actions I'm taking are working.

***Aha moment**: I wanted freedom and flexibility, but I also needed structure, and I had to be more intentional about socializing.*

My workstation in the summer. Summer provides more opportunities to go outside and to socialize!

"Retirement is not in
my vocabulary. They
aren't going to get rid
of me that way."

–Betty White

PART FOUR

Going Beyond My Comfort Zone

"Every day, do something that terrifies you."

- Penny Pennington, Managing Partner Edward Jones Investments.

I was slowly breaking out of my work shell, that shell that makes you careful about what you say, makes you check your true self at the door, and makes you take on a different persona at work.

Besides taking on a different persona at work, I sometimes felt that I had to check my creativity and independent thinking at the door too. Without intending to, I found myself following the unspoken modes of operating and thinking, rarely getting the opportunity to be creative or do something different.

In 2022 I was shedding a lot of that corporate covering and coming into my own. One of the more impactful changes I noticed was that I was becoming more trusting in my instincts, ideas, and decisions. I value getting a second opinion but operating in the corporate world involved a complex dance of getting buy-in on ideas and projects even before you officially presented them as ideas! There were so many checks, balances, and rechecks in place that you were forced to play it safe or risk getting rejected. I didn't realize until recently how that environment had made me more risk-averse, and less trusting in myself.

Aha moment: *after 20 years of typical work life, parts of me had been hibernating and now I had the chance to unleash them again.*

"The 5 Stacks Camp"

It was a Thursday afternoon in summer, and I couldn't have been more excited that the following day was Friday.

"Mom, we did such a good job," my daughter said. I think she could sense that I needed the encouragement and confirmation.

We had just completed our very first financial literacy camp and my daughter, and I breathed a huge sigh of relief.

From Monday to Thursday, twice during the summer of 2022, my then 9-year-old daughter and I hosted groups of 9–12-year-olds at our first The 5 Stacks Camp, where we talk about money and other financial topics with kids.

How did I go from wanting to teach women about investing in the stock market to teaching kids about money?

My thoughts on how The FI Woman could provide value have been evolving, and I was convinced that early financial literacy was an important step to achieving financial independence.

The idea for The 5 Stacks Camp came to me on March 9, 2022. I still remember it vividly.

I woke up in the middle of the night with an idea. There was a knot in the pit of my stomach. I had a big idea. I even thought it was a great idea. I was excited. And afraid. I felt that I needed to spring into action quickly to get the ball rolling, but I also felt a strong urge to do nothing, to stay in the same spot not moving.

I was surprised to find that I was shaking from both excitement and fear. My limbs felt cold.

"I have a great idea." I thought to myself.

"I've had many great ideas, but they haven't yielded the great results I envisioned." I reminded myself.

I had enough of a growth mindset to recognize that I was self-sabotaging.

As far as I knew, there was a gap in teaching about money in schools or even at home, so my idea was to host a virtual summer camp where kids 9-12 could learn about money in a fun way.

But my idea wasn't just for them to learn the basics of money, but to learn about starting a business, investing in the stock market, and being charitable.

I wanted the small class, virtual format to encourage the kids to ask questions and discuss with each other. The main idea was to foster an open learning environment about money.

I knew it was a great idea and a necessity, but I also knew I was outside my comfort zone.

What did I know about working with kids? Would they be interested in learning about money? Would their parents?

Despite my questioning and self-doubt, I knew I was going to take action because I knew that I could not *not* take action.

Once I knew I was going to run with my idea, I sprang into action. That very day I built a webpage and started to publicize the camp.

My daughter and I learned so much. From planning the topics to creating the camp materials, and finally, hosting the camp.

By the time June rolled around for our first set of campers, we were ready, and it was a resounding success! The campers were awesome, engaged, and had fantastic ideas and questions.

Best of all, their parents had wonderful feedback about the camp.

"Thanks. This is phenomenal. H**** really enjoyed the classes. I didn't need to remind him, he logged on to the virtual classes by himself. That is the ultimate sign of authentic engagement for a 10-year-old!

I expected that he would fuss about sitting in a virtual class for 3 hours a day and 4 days this week, but he did not.

Also, he independently shared what he learned with me and his dad every day without being asked. Thank you!!"

The feedback we received was an invaluable gift. The 5 Stacks Camp was truly a passion project, with a mission to engage, empower, and foster early financial literacy.

From a business point of view, we ran the camp at a loss. But it was a worthwhile and fulfilling experience for my daughter and me.

We worked together creating the presentations, preparing camp materials, and she even created a Roblox video that illustrated some money concepts. It was 6 minutes long, and the kids were completely engrossed. She was able to engage the campers at a kid level in a way that I doubt I could have done.

Because she had a say in every aspect of the camp, she was more vested than if I was the only one running the show.

That was one of the important lessons I learned from working with her, letting go of control and trusting her to come up with ideas and a plan.

Working with my daughter taught me how to accept imperfections and let things flow without having a fully baked plan. I am convinced that working with her for one summer taught me more about managing and working with people than years of managing people in the workforce!

Aha moment: *Giving up control, even to a nine-year-old, can produce amazing results!*

An idea to teach kids about money resulted in the birth of The 5 Stacks Camp, which my daughter and I hosted over the summer.

"Embracing the Public"

"It's 2022. Stop hiding your face from the public. Nowadays people NEED to know whom they are buying from!"

This was a message from a very dear sister-friend.

In her own words, she was sick and tired of my desire to hide behind my posts and wanting to be as anonymous as possible. She was right; how could I talk about topics as personal as money and finances, and yet want to remain anonymous?

I didn't enjoy putting myself out there, but I knew she was right about people needing to connect and engage with the people they do business with. They wanted to get personal with you, know you, and know your story. I gritted my teeth and worked at sharing more on social media, telling my story, being vulnerable, and trying to connect more with the public. I was definitely operating way outside of my comfort zone!

I wanted to use my stories to motivate and inspire others, so I started looking for opportunities to get my message out. I was a guest on the Coffee n Tea with S&L podcast where we discussed my journey and helping others thrive financially; I sat down with a great friend for her Confidence Talk and discussed being confident and making bold moves; I was a guest on the Youth P.O.W.E.R podcast where we discussed empowering kids and arming them with financial literacy.

I also had the opportunity to take part in two in-depth articles by well-established organizations.

The first article was conducted by Fidelity Investments as part of a series on FIRE, and it was published in Fidelity Viewpoints. I was one of three people interviewed to share their FIRE journey.

The second article was an interview with SD Voyager. The interview was detailed and focused on my journey from experiencing a layoff from my first job out of college, to achieving my dream of early retirement.

(If you are interested in reading either article, a quick Google search should take you to them.)

The articles are helping me articulate my journey and encourage others on their journey. The more I put myself out there, the more comfortable and confident I become. But it is not easy. I can't control the reaction I get when I share my most vulnerable stories, or wholeheartedly share information that I think will help others. I don't know who is genuinely interested in my journey or who is just looking for an opportunity to poke holes at it and tear it down. I can't control how people receive my message, but I am determined to keep sharing it.

Aha moment: *stepping out of one's comfort zone is uncomfortable, but the longer you stay there, the more comfortable you become.*

PART FIVE

Finally, Getting the Hang of It!

One of the best things that have happened since retiring is going on this entrepreneurial journey with my childhood friend.

She isn't retired, but she made the huge decision to leave her executive position in corporate America to become a confidence coach and change management consultant.

I imagine that my retirement would have been a lot lonelier and more isolating if she hadn't made that decision.

It first started with Monday calls to "check in" and stay accountable for the things we wanted to accomplish: me, getting The FI Woman running smoothly and understanding what I wanted to accomplish with it, and her, refining her value proposition for her clients and future business model.

Today, we meet almost every day! Tuesdays and Thursdays to complete a YouTube workout, Mondays, Wednesdays, and Fridays to talk business, stay accountable, and exchange ideas. Without this intentional, and constant point of contact, it would have been very challenging to stay motivated or positive during the past year of retirement.

Besides this much-needed external contact, I started to get the hang of retirement in other important ways too.

"I was at Barnes & Noble, and I consciously decided not to buy a book that I loved at first sight!"

I was talking to a friend and trying to impress upon her why this was such a monumental step for me.

I have a few "bad" money habits that I am trying to come to grips with in retirement. One of them is curbing unplanned purchases, especially for books and experiences.

I can always justify why I need another book, or why that show is once-in-a-lifetime. The other is paying closer attention to prices and bargain shopping.

This is especially true for groceries, my twice-annual clothes shopping, and gas.

In the past, my sister has looked at me incredulously when I told her I didn't always look at the price of the clothes I picked off the rack until I got to the cash register, or that I didn't know how much gas cost.

Let me explain because I don't want to come across as an entitled, unaware, privileged person. I'll begin with the explanation I gave my sister.

"When I go shopping, I know the stores I can afford. I shop based on what I need, what fits, and what looks nice; and since I'm in a shop I know is affordable, I'm not expecting any surprises."

She listened to my explanation, but she didn't seem very impressed by it!

It's a similar explanation for gas. I need the gas, regardless of the price, and since I don't want to drive to several gas stations looking for the cheapest price, I stop at the nearest gas station and fill up.

"What about your budget?" was one of the questions my sister asked.

Ah, my budget.

A definite lesson learned in retirement; my budget needed to be a lot tighter! Before retiring, my budget consisted of "buckets" and physically segregating my money by using multiple bank accounts. It's a very effective strategy for making your spending visible and helping you stick to a budget.

Side note: I had my money in up to twenty-one different accounts at one point! Online banks are great for physically segregating your money.

Budgeting for me meant that I assigned an amount to categories of items based on my analysis of my previous spending. I tried to put as many expenses as possible on a schedule, for example, clothes shopping twice a year so that I could better plan how I spent my money. Then, when I needed to spend from that category, it was easy to stick to the budget, as long as prices had not drastically changed.

Before retiring, I could afford to occasionally 'rob Peter to pay Paul' because I had a renewable source to replenish from. But since retiring, that source is fixed and depleting, which has forced me to rethink the way I budget.

My annual income pre-retirement was $155K excluding benefits and bonuses. My planned income in retirement is $40K. That's about a quarter of my pre-retirement income. While my retirement income is sufficient for covering my expenses, including planned fun activities, it is not sufficient for (or designed to) cover last-minute, unplanned expenses.

I realized I was going to have to learn a new set of financial mindsets that were different from the ones that got me to early retirement.

Aha moment: the money mindsets that helped me achieve early retirement might not be the same mindsets I need to succeed in retirement.

The fear and struggle of "wasting time" is real. My head is filled with all the admonitions of how valuable time is, and how once spent, it can never be regained.

I worry about getting bored, losing focus, or losing motivation for my beloved business. I have also struggled with a loss of identity.

Like most people, part of my identity comes from what I do, my accomplishments, and even how much I earn. Now that I am retired, what is my identity?

I know that every phase in life brings a new journey of self-discovery, and I am gaining insights about myself and my new sense of identity.

One year into retirement and I feel I am finally finding a balanced way to enjoy my newfound freedom, while being mindful not squander it! When I first retired, I still had that need to move fast, complete tasks, and accomplish things, all at breakneck speed. Now I can slow the pace and still get important things done.

Aha moment: *retirement can bring about a sense of loss of identity, but it is also a great opportunity to reflect, learn about yourself, and come up with a new identity.*

EPILOGUE

What's Next?

"What is a legacy? It's planting seeds in a garden you never get to see."

- Lin-Manuel Miranda, playwright

One year after retirement and I have gained insights and experiences from having the freedom to explore different paths and expand my network.

I have become accustomed to being in control of my time, and although the fear of having to "unretire" is real, I don't see myself ever going back to the 9 to 5 way of life.

Running The FI Woman is a challenge that I am enjoying so much! Even though I don't need to earn a living, I still feel the pressure all entrepreneurs feel to create a successful and lasting business. On more than one occasion my daughter has said that when she grows up, she would like to take over my business. That's serious motivation for me!

I want to provide value and leave a lasting legacy.

Lin-Manuel Miranda, the playwright, described legacy as "planting seeds in a garden you never get to see."

I want to plant the seeds of financial independence and financial literacy in as many "gardens" as I can.

When I started The FI Woman, I wanted it to become a call to action, a movement for women to take control of their money and gain financial independence. It's the driving force behind many of the things that I do and hope to do in the future. I have never really seen myself as the type of person to leave a legacy or even have the desire to do so. It always seemed like such an "old person" thing to do or something only "great" people did.

Now, I realize that legacy isn't about being old or great; it's about planting seeds, and with The FI Woman, I hope to plant many seeds that grow to lift a generation of people financially.

Legacy is planting seeds in a garden you never get to see.

THE END

♡♡

Made in United States
Troutdale, OR
11/03/2026

56852535R00069